Original title:
Cracking Up in the Clearing

Copyright © 2025 Creative Arts Management OÜ
All rights reserved.

Author: Miriam Kensington
ISBN HARDBACK: 978-1-80567-351-4
ISBN PAPERBACK: 978-1-80567-650-8

Mischievous Moments in the Emerald Haven

In the glen where shadows play,
Squirrels dance the night away.
They steal acorns, what a show,
Chasing tails, then off they go.

A rabbit with a too-cool grin,
Wears a hat—oh, where to begin?
He hops along, with flair and glee,
As if he's hosting a grand tea spree.

A fox with boots, a sight to see,
Jumps in puddles, wild and free.
His friends all laugh, they roll with mirth,
Creating chaos in their girth.

With each giggle, the trees all sway,
Mirroring the fun at play.
Nature's laughter fills the air,
In this haven, joy is rare.

Celestial Chimes Amidst the Tall Pines

Under stars that twinkle bright,
Owl conducts the band tonight.
A midnight tune, a comical flare,
The forest joins with giggles rare.

A raccoon juggles fruit with ease,
Tomatoes rolling, oh, what a tease!
He winks and spins, then takes a bow,
The crowd erupts; it's fun, oh wow!

A lizard in a polka-dot hat,
Twirls and twirls, imagine that!
He trips, he flips, but lands with style,
The audience roars, what a while!

At dawn, the antics fade away,
Left are echoes of yesterday.
But come the night, with stars so bright,
The forest knows it's time for flight.

Echoes of Delighted Whimsy

In the meadow, shadows sway,
Silly critters come to play.
A rabbit wears a daring hat,
While the turtle dances like a brat.

Laughter echoes, wild and free,
A squirrel spins a joke, you see.
With winks and nods, they jest and tease,
Nature giggles in the breeze.

Fractured Smiles in Bloom

Petals burst in vibrant cheer,
While bees buzz jokes we all can hear.
A sunflower grins, so tall and bright,
Tickling leaves with sheer delight.

Bunnies hop with comical flair,
Chasing shadows without a care.
Each bloom a giggle, each bud a jest,
In this joyous garden, we find our rest.

Frolic in the Glade

Dancing shadows in the glade,
A frog jumps high, a wild charade.
Whirling leaves come down like twirls,
As wind spirits tease the tiny pearls.

A dandelion whispers a pun,
While ants march by, just having fun.
Each corner calls for laughter's grace,
Together we find our funny place.

Chortles Beneath the Canopy

Underneath the leafy arc,
A group of squirrels makes their mark.
With a thump, a nut goes rolling,
Amidst the laughter, there's no controlling.

Branches twist and branches knot,
Creating laughter on the spot.
As critters giggle, the sun shines bright,
In this wonderland of pure delight.

Revelry at the Edge of the Trail

Frogs are croaking like they're in a band,
A raccoon tiptoes, shuffling in the sand.
Squirrels debate, should they stash or share,
While a bobcat watches with a curious stare.

Laughter tumbles through the sun-dappled trees,
As chipmunks giggle, tumbling with ease.
One slips and flips, strikes a pose so grand,
While the forest chuckles, nature's own stand.

Smirking Shadows in the Undergrowth

Mice gaming with leaves, they think they're so sly,
As shadows sprout grins, a wink in the sky.
A crow caws loudly, it's nuts they require,
While a lizard sunbathes, a bit of a liar.

Ferns wave hello, gossiping with glee,
Whispers of mischief, as wild as can be.
A rabbit fumbles, trips over its feet,
Under watchful giggles, the day feels sweet.

Delightful Fracas in the Open Air

A butterfly waltzes in a graceful dance,
While bumblebees buzz, seizing their chance.
Petals are fluttering, a dress-up affair,
In this delightful chaos, all are aware.

Crickets play games, chirping loud and clear,
As ants march in lines, full of good cheer.
A dog joins the fun, chasing shadows around,
In this wacky setting, joy knows no bound.

Playful Banter by the Stream

Water splashes loudly, like giggles afloat,
Fish dart and dive, in a slippery boat.
A moose drops by, with an elegant glance,
While ducks quack away in a bubbly dance.

Rocks chatter softly, sharing their views,
On the antics of frogs in their splashing shoes.
With each ripple's laugh, the sunlight beams,
Whispering tales of comical dreams.

Serenity Offbeat in Nature's Theatre

In the glade where shadows play,
A squirrel juggles acorns today.
Birds wear hats, they strut and sway,
While frogs keep time in a ballet.

The trees applaud with rustling leaves,
A raccoon dons their finest sleeves.
With each laugh, the world receives,
Nature's stage, where mirth believes.

Laughter Lit in the Bright Green

A bee buzzed by with a giggling spin,
While daisies whispered, 'Let's begin!'
The sun played tricks with a cheeky grin,
As clouds conspired with laughter thin.

Ants marched on, like a marching band,
Twirling spots in the soft, warm sand.
They danced around, as if they planned,
To take the crown of mirth firsthand.

Fanciful Tales from the Leafy Canvas

A fox in glasses reads a tome,
As butterflies serve tea and foam.
The trees are scribes, in emerald dome,
Collecting stories, nature's home.

A rabbit quips with witty flair,
While lizards bask without a care.
In this odd world, laughter's rare,
Yet blooms like flowers in the air.

Peals of Laughter Through the Trees

A chipmunk danced upon a log,
With funny steps, it wiggled, jogged.
The breeze blew tales as dense as fog,
With every laugh, it felt like a smog.

Woodpeckers knock with jolly beats,
As rabbits plot in funny feats.
Nature sings in silly treats,
Where each day starts with cheerful tweets.

Riddles in the Rustic Retreat

In the woods where shadows play,
Trees whisper secrets, come what may.
A squirrel wore socks, quite bizarre,
    Chasing after a runaway jar.

The owls host parties, what a sight!
With disco balls and moonlight bright.
The raccoons tap dance, oh so slick,
In their party hats, they dance and stick.

A frog recites poetry with flair,
While crickets strum tunes without a care.
All the critters share a good cheer,
    Laughter echoes, far and near.

So come to this spot, where joy ignites,
And riddles unfold in twinkling nights.
In the clearing, where whimsy thrives,
    Nature giggles, and laughter survives.

Laughter Blooms in the Forest's Heart

Near the brook where wildflowers sway,
A bear does ballet, in such a way!
His tutu's bright, his moves a laugh,
Join the crowd for the best autograph!

Bunnies juggle carrots with grace,
While hedgehogs play chess, embracing their space.
Flowers wear hats, oh what a sight!
A parade of joy in the soft moonlight.

The woodpeckers sing a comical tune,
As fireflies dance under the shining moon.
With giggles and grins, all gather round,
In this vibrant place, pure joy is found.

So let's toast with acorns, raise them high,
Laughter blossoms beneath this sky.
In this heart of the forest, life's a playful art,
Every corner alive with humor's heart.

Amusement in the Arboretum

Under branches of twisting vines,
A fox tells tales, full of punchlines.
With a wink and a grin, he spins each yarn,
The merriment spreads like a live barn.

Trees wear glasses, oh how they read!
The stories of joy, they all just need.
A bobcat crochets, with claws so neat,
Stitching up giggles, a sight so sweet.

Squirrels race on a tightrope high,
While mushrooms giggle as they pass by.
The cool breeze carries a chuckle or two,
A festival of laughter, bright and new.

In this arboretum where joy is found,
Every leaf rustles with laughter's sound.
Join the fun, let your worries flee,
In this wild retreat, we're all so free.

Whimsy Within the Wilderness

In the clearing where mischief grows,
A canyon echoing laughter flows.
Grasshoppers leap with a comic twist,
Dancing with daisies, you can't resist.

A goat wearing sneakers, rambunctious and spry,
Challenges birds to a race in the sky.
Fields of giggles roll and tumble,
As sunlight catches the joyous rumble.

Chasing shadows, the crew breaks out,
Hopscotch with dandelions, hear them shout!
The playful wind adds its voice to the cheer,
Bringing the fun and tickling the ear.

In this dear wilderness, whimsy breeds,
Laughter at every turn, in smiles and seeds.
Join the raucous, the frolicsome scheme,
For in this land, all life is a dream.

Laughter in the Meadow

Bouncing bunnies hop around,
Chasing shadows on the ground.
Tickling grass beneath their feet,
Laughter echoes, oh so sweet.

A squirrel slipped on a pine cone,
Land of giggles, never alone.
Frogs in chorus, croak and tease,
Nature's joke puts me at ease.

Whispers Among the Pines

Pines stand tall, whispering jokes,
Breezes laugh with gentle pokes.
A cheeky chipmunk takes the stage,
His antics fill the woods with rage.

Sunlight dances, shadows play,
Laughter joins the light ballet.
The forest hums a playful tune,
Nature's laughter, morning to noon.

Bursting with Joyful Echoes

Daisies sway, a cheerful choir,
Their laughter lifts us, never tire.
From daisies bright to skies so blue,
Each giggle feels like morning dew.

Bubbles float and burst in flight,
Ticklish tickles spark delight.
With every bounce, my heart does soar,
Life's a party, who could ask for more?

Sunlit Giggles

Sunbeams tickle all around,
Laughing leaves make a joyful sound.
Children chase the clouds above,
Spreading giggles, sharing love.

Butterflies join in the fun,
Twisting, turning, oh what a run!
Each giggle floats upon the air,
In this moment, joy we share.

Kooky Beats in the Nature Tune

In the forest, squirrels grooved,
Twisting tails, they danced and moved.
A rabbit tripped, fell on a stack,
Then bounced right up, no grace to lack.

The flowers swayed like they were high,
Bees buzzing tunes that made us sigh.
A frog in shades croaked out some beats,
Gathering critters with silly feats.

The breeze played jokes with leaves that spun,
Whispering laughter, oh what fun!
A toadstool stage for all to see,
Where all our worries ceased to be.

So join the merry woodland crew,
We'll laugh and dance beneath skies blue.
Nature's rhythm fills the air,
In this kooky beat, joy's everywhere.

Japes in the Glittering Glade

In the glade where shadows shift,
Bouncing berries, nature's gift.
A hedgehog wore a flower crown,
Prancing 'round without a frown.

The sunlight winked through leafy beams,
Whispered secrets, spun our dreams.
A chicken strutted, stole a show,
With clucks and quacks as laughter flowed.

Mushrooms giggled, patches bright,
Tickling toes, such pure delight.
A fox flipped tricks, oh what a sight,
Under the moon, they danced all night.

In this place where play is rife,
With nature's jest, we share our life.
In the glimmer, joy cascades,
With every chuckle, love invades.

Vibrant Tidings from the Earth Mother

The earth mother whispers soft and clear,
Her vibrant tales always near.
With giggles sprouting from the ground,
A world of wonders we have found.

Her flowers wink; they bloom with cheer,
As playful breezes lift our spirits here.
A gnome with antics, all in style,
Locks of moss, oh what a smile.

The laughter echoes past the trees,
Bouncing back on the summer breeze.
A turtle tells a joke, so sly,
As birds above just swoop on by.

With every twist of nature's weave,
From lively sprouts, we all believe.
These vibrant tidings, joyous prance,
Unite us all in joyful dance.

Joy Cascading in the Waning Light

As daylight drips like melting ice,
The meadow laughs, oh so precise.
A firefly named Ziggy danced,
In sparkly shoes, it pranced and pranced.

Bunnies put on a comedy play,
Telling tales throughout the day.
While crickets sang the evening tune,
We laughed along with the glowing moon.

A raccoon juggled acorns with flair,
As raccoons often do without a care.
Winking stars in a velvet sky,
A wish sat nestled in our eye.

In waning light, our spirits lift,
Nature's joy, the greatest gift.
With every giggle, a story flows,
In all our hearts, the laughter grows.

Mirthful Moments in the Hollow

In the woods where giggles sprout,
Squirrels wear hats, there's no doubt.
A rabbit laughs, then starts to sway,
As mushrooms dance in a silly fray.

Leaves chuckle low, tickling the breeze,
While ants march to tunes, oh so pleased.
A jolly frog leaps in a jest,
Spreading joy in this leafy nest.

Sunbeams wink from the tree tops bright,
As shadows play hide and seek with light.
Laughter bubbles like water in streams,
In this hollow, we all chase dreams.

With every twirl, the forest grins,
Silly plays where fun never thins.
So join the fray, let spirits fly,
In this mirth, we can't deny.

Glee Thriving in Nature's Embrace

Breezes whisper secrets of jest,
While flowers giggle, never at rest.
Bees buzz softly, sharing a laugh,
Drawing smiles on each leafy path.

A happy tree shakes its leafy mane,
As squirrels play tag through sunshine and rain.
With every rustle, there's joy to share,
In nature's embrace, all worries are rare.

The brook chuckles with mischievous schemes,
Carrying stories from whimsical dreams.
A fox spins tales of his wild pranks,
While ducks quack humor in joyful ranks.

In every corner, cheer does unfold,
Life in the woods is a tale retold.
So laugh aloud, let your spirit play,
In nature's arms, we dance and sway.

Hushed Chuckles in the Green Oasis

In the shade where secrets spill,
Gentle whispers give a thrill.
Beneath the ferns, a frog makes jokes,
Sending ripples through crowding oaks.

Bumblebees tease with buzz and dance,
While daisies grin at a flower's chance.
The sun peeks through with a wink so sly,
Catching giggles as moments fly.

A wise old owl, perched in delight,
Tells puns to stars that twinkle at night.
The wind carries laughter, soft and bold,
In this green oasis, stories unfold.

So take a seat, let the fun begin,
Nature's carefree, let the laughs spin.
In hushed tones, joy weaves through the leaves,
In this refuge, our spirit believes.

Jolly Tempests in the Clearing

When winds play tricks, the trees all sway,
As blossoms giggle and drift away.
Clouds join in with playful might,
Turning the day into silly fright.

Raindrops bounce like kids on the run,
Turning puddles into laughter and fun.
A dog spins round, chasing its tail,
In this jolly mess, we can't fail.

The sun peeks out and starts to grin,
As raindrops join in with happy din.
Wildflowers dance in their colorful skirts,
Poking fun at the sky's little spurts.

So here in the clearing, we frolic and play,
Letting go of worries, come what may.
Jolly tempests, in their wild delight,
Create a canvas of pure-hearted light.

Exuberant Whirls on the Forest Floor

A squirrel danced with a mighty flair,
Spinning 'round without a single care.
Leaves flew up in a twirling spree,
Nature giggled with wild glee.

A rabbit joined with an eager leap,
Bounding 'round in a hop so deep.
Mice created a raucous beat,
As branches swayed to the silly feat.

Frogs leapt high like they knew the tune,
Croaking loudly under the moon.
Each creature wore a zany grin,
As the fun and frolic did begin.

With every twirl and every jig,
They found joy in a world so big.
Nature's laughter echoed through,
As the whimsy spread like morning dew.

Blissful Jests in the Woodland Clearing

In a sunny spot where the wildflowers grow,
A bear wore shades and took center show.
With a funky hat and a dance so spry,
The woodland critters laughed, oh my!

A fox in a bowtie played the flute,
While a clever raccoon shook his boot.
Chirps and giggles filled the warm air,
As trees leaned in to see the affair.

The chipmunks clapped with tiny paws,
At the antics of their funny cause.
With every twirl upon the grass,
The woodland's mirth just seemed to amass.

Hiccups from laughter bounced all around,
As joy took flight without a bound.
With winks and humor, they did unite,
In that comfy clearing, basking in light.

Twilight Jinks at Nature's Edge

Under twilight skies so warm and bright,
A hedgehog waddled in a comical sight.
With tiny glasses perched on his nose,
He slipped and stumbled but struck a pose.

Fireflies flickered, playing tag,
As a kite-loving rabbit shared a brag.
With wings made of leaves, oh what a flight,
They zipped through shadows in pure delight.

Owl chimed in with a wisecrack or two,
While crickets laughed in a merry crew.
The grass shimmied with giggles galore,
As the twilight jinks opened wide their door.

Nature chuckled, her heart so light,
With every jest as day turned to night.
They danced till stars began to peek,
In a merry minuet, their spirits unique.

Daffy Moments in the Meadow's Glow

In a meadow bright with daisies and sun,
A frog in a bowler had too much fun.
He leaped and he croaked a silly song,
As the daisies swayed and hummed along.

A dandy lion and his buddy bee,
Had a race that stirred the sweet honey tree.
With buzzing laughter and a playful chase,
They rolled in the clover, a joyous race.

The bouncy bunnies hopped to a beat,
Performing stunts no one could beat.
With dippy dances and zany spins,
They brought forth the laughter that never thins.

As the sunset painted the meadow's best,
The critters gathered for one big jest.
With silly songs as the day bid adieu,
They celebrated life, all merry and new.

Jests of Nature in the Thicket

Squirrels in a mad dash, a playful race,
Chasing tails in a frenzied embrace.
Rabbits share jokes, oh what a delight,
While trees shake their leaves, joining the light.

A chipmunk sneezes, a fluttering scene,
Butterflies giggle at the sight, quite keen.
Hawks above chuckle, they wink as they soar,
Nature's a jester, always wanting more.

Hilarity Sprouts Among the Ferns

Frogs croak in chorus, a ribbiting band,
Dance like no one's watching, the floor is the land.
Mice crack up, tickled by leaves that tickle,
As the sun plays a tune, oh what a fickle!

A lizard slips, wearing a hat made of dew,
In this silly party, everyone's in the queue.
The ferns sway in laughter, they wiggle with glee,
In this merry woodland, all are carefree.

Tension Unwinds in the Grove

Tall trees stand tall, but they can't interfere,
While owls spin tales that make all of them cheer.
Breezes whisper secrets, a ticklish affair,
As shadows twirl round, engaging in flair.

A bear drops a picnic, oh what a mess,
Bees buzz with laughter, no need to impress.
As light slowly fades, the giggles take flight,
In the grove of delight, oh what a sight!

Giggles Beneath the Boughs

Under branches low, laughter hangs in the air,
With each gentle swing, joy's everywhere.
A family of foxes plays a prancing game,
While the wind whistles tunes, it's all quite the same.

The grass grows taller, ticks tickle the toes,
While daisies nod softly, as if sharing prose.
Amid shadows and light, the world finds its cheer,
Underneath the boughs, all hearts draw near.

Playful Breezes

A squirrel wears a tiny hat,
It dances on the garden mat.
The teasing winds blow here and there,
As laughter floats upon the air.

A butterfly drinks from a soda,
While ants march in a funny moda.
They trade tall tales of yesterday,
In the sunshine, they laugh and play.

The trees wiggle with glee today,
Their branches bend in a silly sway.
A robin tells a joke so sly,
While clouds giggle as they float by.

With every gust, a chuckle brews,
Nature's jesters all come to muse.
In this bright patch of endless cheer,
The world spins round, no room for tear.

Celestial Chuckles

Stars wink at the moon's bright face,
A comet zips in a light race.
Galaxies weave tales up high,
While stardust drips like candy pie.

The sun wears shades with style and flair,
And sunscreens share a sunny dare.
Planets spin in a merry whirl,
As laughter echoes, a cosmic twirl.

Asteroids toss their rocky jokes,
And giggles start from spacey folks.
Saturn's rings do cha-cha slides,
As everyone in space confides.

In this vast, much lighted sphere,
Laughter brakes all doubt and fear.
Under skies that glow and beam,
The universe is one big dream.

Mirth in the Open Air

A kite dances, a vibrant sight,
It flaps and flutters, pure delight.
Children giggle as it soars,
Shouting tales of playful wars.

The grass tickles as they roll,
Belly laughs bounce, heart and soul.
Bubbles float on breezy trails,
Pop! The joy never fails.

A picnic feast, a grand parade,
Sandwiches stacked, lemonade made.
A dog steals a slice of cake,
And everyone joins the belly ache.

In this place where laughter reigns,
Every moment, joy maintains.
The sun dips low with a wink,
In the open air, we never sink.

Joy Unbound

A jester walks beneath the trees,
With floppy shoes and antics, he sees.
He juggles fruits of many hues,
While everyone sings silly blues.

A goat in boots starts to prance,
With every leap, it takes a chance.
The crowd erupts in hearty cheers,
As laughter dances through the years.

A picnic's spread, a feast so grand,
Every bite by laughter planned.
The ants join in, all in a row,
Carrying crumbs, stealing the show.

With smiles bright and hearts aglow,
In this land where good vibes flow.
Joy unbound in every sound,
In every moment, bliss is found.

Chortles Amidst the Thickets

In the thicket, giggles bloom,
Squirrels join in silly tune.
Wobbling branches, a dance so spry,
A rustle here, a snicker nigh.

Frogs wear hats of leafy grace,
Bouncing thoughts, a merry chase.
Butterflies chuckle, flotillas bright,
As flowers gossip, full of light.

In the nooks, where shadows play,
Laughter lingers, come what may.
A hedgehog spins, lost in the fun,
While daisies wink at everyone.

Nature's jesters, wild and free,
Crafting joy, a jubilee.
With every twist, a prank takes flight,
In thickets lush, all feels just right.

Tongue-in-Cheek Beneath the Tree Crown

Under the tree, where shadows burst,
Whispers of humor, oh how they thirst!
Parrots mimic a silly tune,
Beneath the glow of a jocular moon.

A raccoon juggles acorns round,
While laughter echoes, a happy sound.
Swaying branches do a jig,
The whole scene's one big, merry gig.

Mice in boots march with delight,
Their tiny moves a comical sight.
Even the roots hum a song,
In this quirky grove, we all belong.

With every chuckle, spirits soar,
A patch of joy, forevermore.
Beneath the trees, mischief plays,
In nature's jest, we lose our ways.

Delightful Whirls in the Whispering Woods

In whispering woods, where giggles grow,
Twisted paths, with crafty flow.
A deer pretends to knight a crow,
With mismatched horns, a comical show.

Leaves flutter down like laughing sprites,
Tickling noses as each one alights.
The wind tells jokes with a playful gust,
Bringing smiles, it's a must.

Bumbles and giggles painted in green,
A world of whimsy, unexpected scene.
The brook is chuckling, dancing light,
With all its ripples, pure delight.

Nature's jest never gets old,
Stories of laughter, brightly told.
In every corner, chuckles appear,
A symphony of joy, ringing clear.

Jolly Fractals of Nature's Design

Fractals swirl in laughter's thread,
Patterns weaving what joy has spread.
The flowers wink, a colorful tease,
While bees get dizzy, buzzing with ease.

Twirling branches, a playful jest,
In the meadow's heart, we find our rest.
A fox wears spectacles, quite absurd,
With each step closer, we chuckle unheard.

The rivers giggle, tickling the stones,
Echoes of laughter in playful tones.
A parade of critters, so sprightly aligned,
In nature's jest, true joy you'll find.

With every leaf and every breeze,
Joy is woven through trees and seas.
Crafted in humor, the world spins round,
In these jolly patterns, love is found.

Lively Reverberations of Joy

In the woods where giggles bloom,
Trees sway in a playful tune.
Mushrooms dance in mismatched shoes,
Squirrels chuckle, sharing news.

Butterflies wear hats of glee,
Bouncing on breezes, wild and free.
Laughter rolls like a river grand,
Joy painting all across the land.

Crickets join with their silly songs,
Joking about where each bug belongs.
The sun winks, a playful tease,
As flowers nod in the gentle breeze.

Each shadow holds a quirky tale,
Of merry critters on a trail.
Lively echoes bounce and race,
In this wild, whimsical space.

Sassy Sprouts in the Green Haven

Beneath the leaves where sass takes flight,
Sassy sprouts bask in the light.
Whimsical whispers, a jovial spree,
Chasing daisies, can't catch me!

Wiggly worms with a sly little grin,
Swinging on roots where the fun begins.
Dandelions puff with such flair,
Sprouting giggles in the air.

Frogs croak jokes from lily pads bright,
Their humor hopping with pure delight.
A breeze tickles the grass so low,
Each blade laughing, putting on a show.

In this vivid, verdant ground,
Joyful whispers are all around.
Each moment bursts with playful cheer,
In our little green haven, so dear.

Gleeful Whispering in the Verdant Silence

In quiet woods where laughter stirs,
Gleeful whispers, nature purrs.
Ferns giggle under the moon's soft light,
While shadows prance in the starry night.

A raccoon jests with a stolen snack,
Mischief dancing along its back.
Leaves rustle with a cheeky song,
In this secret world where all belong.

Treetops sway with a gentle tease,
As owls chuckle as they please.
Rabbits hop in a comical chase,
In this hidden, happy place.

The stream chuckles over stones,
Murmuring tales in playful tones.
In the hush, the laughter's loud,
In verdant silence, we stand proud.

Humor in the Roots of Serenity

Deep in the soil where laughter grows,
Roots mingle with glee, it surely shows.
Beneath the calm, a riot unfolds,
Stories of joy, daring and bold.

Ants parade with their tiny snacks,
Cracking jokes in their little packs.
A wise old tree leans in to hear,
Each punchline shared brings good cheer.

Blades swish like whispers of jest,
As critters play hopscotch, feeling blessed.
The breeze carries giggles on its backs,
In this peaceful place where humor cracks.

Serenity hugs us, warm and tight,
Yet beneath, a giggle takes flight.
In the roots, where quiet reigns,
Humor blooms in delicious gains.

Treading Lightly on Laughter

In the woods where giggles play,
Footsteps dance in a silly sway.
Leaves whisper secrets, oh so sly,
Bubbles burst as the butterflies fly.

Grass tickles toes, a merry tease,
Nature chuckles in the soft breeze.
Squirrels prance with a cheeky grin,
Chasing shadows, let the fun begin!

Sunbeams wiggle through the trees,
Casting spells that aim to please.
Echoes of joy bounce off the bark,
Inviting laughter, igniting the spark.

Peeking mushrooms, round and stout,
Join the jest, let laughter sprout.
In the clearing, joy unfurls,
Beneath the dance of merry twirls.

The Lightness of Being

Floating on whispers of light,
Giggling squirrels sprout delight.
Each ray of sun a gentle tease,
Breezes chuckle, put you at ease.

Patches of joy scatter around,
Joyful footsteps make a sound.
Wandering thoughts in the air,
Bouncing laughter everywhere.

Clouds tease blue skies with a grin,
Tickling faces, let's begin.
Nature winks in playful spree,
Reminding us how light can be.

In this place where laughter sprains,
Even the sun has silly pains.
And as we tread, just so free,
Being light is the key, you see!

Susurrations of Merriment

Whispers of joy in the rustling leaves,
Dancing along with the playful eaves.
Every blade of grass joined in glee,
Painting laughter, wild and free.

Chirps and chuckles fill the air,
Bouncing bubbles, no room for despair.
Breezes tickling a nearby stream,
Sparking giggles, like a dream.

Fluttering wings in a grand ballet,
Spreading smiles along the way.
Sunshine wraps us, warm and bright,
Every moment, pure delight.

Golden laughter dances at dawn,
Drawing circles on the green lawn.
Nature's jest in every nook,
Spinning humor in every book.

Wildflower Whimsy

Where wildflowers laugh in a bloom,
Dandelions drift through the room.
Each petal's giggle a soft caress,
Mirthful dreams in their colorful dress.

Bumblebees buzzing a cheerful tune,
Leading a waltz under the moon.
Frolicking petals, soft and spry,
Painting the world as they flutter by.

The sky spills laughter, rosy and red,
Ticklish clouds raising their head.
Joyful colors swirl and twirl,
In this arena, laughter unfurls.

With each step, a wild dance grows,
Blossoms chuckle where the wind blows.
This clearing plays a merry role,
Delivering joy for the soul.

Gleeful Hiccups in the Nature's Breath

In the meadow, voices chirp,
A hiccup breaks, a tiny burp.
Grasshoppers dance, the breeze is light,
Giggling shadows, a silly sight.

Butterflies waltz with flowers bright,
A sneeze, a laugh, pure delight.
Nature chuckles in boundless cheer,
It's hard not to smile when friends are near.

Rabbits hop with their fluffy tails,
Chasing each other with funny wails.
Sunbeams trickle, laughter flows,
Every corner, joy just grows.

Bouncing bubbles, tickle fights,
Under the stars, laughing nights.
Nature's laughter, a bubbling stream,
In this cheerful world, we dream.

Laughter Fluttering on the Twilight Wind

The evening sun starts to dip,
We giggle and stumble, a charming trip.
Crickets sing in a quirky tune,
As fireflies jiggle by the moon.

On the trail, a squirrel leaps,
With each tiny sound, our laughter seeps.
Giggly echoes fill the air,
Nature joins in, without a care.

A quick trip on a mossy log,
Amidst the laughter, a playful fog.
Suddenly tripped by a sneaky vine,
Together we burst into laughter divine.

Twilight whispers with gentle zest,
Every chuckle, a nature's jest.
Life's a game, in this perfect blend,
With laughter as our joyful friend.

Joyful Encounters in the Woodland Cleansing

Among the trees, a whimsy chase,
Leaves rustle as we break the space.
A startled deer gives us a look,
Its surprised hop — oh, what a hook!

Ferns tickle as we swiftly glide,
Laughter mingles with the forest wide.
A fallen branch, we both misread,
In a comical tumble, two friends proceed.

Sunlight dapples through the green,
Playful antics keep our spirits keen.
A sudden splash in the cool, clear brook,
Giggles echo — what a funny nook!

Every branch has a story shared,
In this woodland, naught is spared.
Joyful moments, wild and free,
Nature's laugh, our melody.

Frolicsome Delights in Nature's Heart

Amidst the meadows, laughter blooms,
Silly hats, an orchestra of tunes.
Wobbly walks on the grassy hills,
Nature smiles with its playful thrills.

A breezy dance makes us twirl,
With every dip, we laugh and swirl.
A snappy branch catches our hats,
We tumble back, make silly spats.

With daisies and dandelions entwined,
A funny face, our minds aligned.
Each rustle and chirp invites a cheer,
Frolicsome joys are gathered near.

Every rustle sings a tune,
To frolic and giggle under the moon.
Nature's heart pulses in delight,
As we share our laughter through the night.

Revelry in the Wild

Amidst the trees, a squirrel danced,
Wiggling its tail in a funny prance.
A cackle of birds joined in the cheer,
Nature's comedy, loud and clear.

A fox with a hat, a sight so rare,
Tipped it to friends with flair to spare.
Laughter echoed through the glade,
While a bear juggled fruit, unafraid.

The sun peeked through with a cheeky smile,
Bouncing light on leaves, let's pause a while.
A deer slipped on moss, fell in a heap,
Nature giggled, no time for sleep.

In this woodsy world of fun and jest,
Every creature is simply blessed.
With a wink and a wiggle, let's all unite,
Revelry and joy from morning to night.

Daydreams of Delight

A rabbit rode a bicycle fast,
With carrots in tow, a sight unsurpassed.
It waved to the ants, marching in line,
"Join my parade, it's going to shine!"

Clouds drifted by, wearing silly hats,
While bees played drums like jazzy brats.
Rainbows slid down like a slide from above,
Whispering secrets of laughter and love.

A turtle played checkers with a wise owl,
As laughter erupted, the trees took a growl.
Sprinkling joy like confetti in spring,
Dreams were as light as the songbirds could sing.

With every giggle, the world felt right,
Daydreams of wonder danced in the light.
Join the fun, leave your worries behind,
For joy in the wild is what we will find!

Blossoms of Joyful Chaos

In a garden where humor takes flight,
Petunias danced under the moonlight.
Tulips wore socks that were mismatched,
As the night's story lovingly scratched.

A bee in sunglasses buzzed with flair,
Chased by a cat who thought it was rare.
Daisies giggled in a pastel parade,
While the sun chuckled, unafraid.

Frogs leaped with joy on lily pads tight,
Creating a symphony of giggles each night.
Roses exchanged jokes with grinning weeds,
In this garden, laughter plants seeds.

With blossoms of joy in every nook,
Nature writes tales in every book.
Let chaos reign with a giggle or two,
For in this wild bloom, there's magic in view!

Soundtrack of Serendipity

In the forest, a melody played,
Made of giggles and mischief displayed.
A raccoon, the DJ, spun tunes so fine,
As critters danced, forming a line.

The wind whispered secrets with a laugh,
Tickling leaves, like a playful staff.
The brook hummed a jovial beat,
And the stars joined in with a twinkling greet.

A parrot cracked jokes with a cheeky flair,
Sipping on nectar without a care.
Every hop and flap made a sound,
A delightful rhythm, joyous and round.

In this wild symphony of delight,
Serendipity soared into the night.
Tune into laughter, let happiness reign,
For a soundtrack like this is utterly insane!

Amusing Revelations in the Leafy Nook

In the nook where squirrels jest,
They plot and scheme, never rest.
With acorns flying high and wide,
Their little jokes, they cannot hide.

A rabbit hops, a grin so wide,
As leaves come tumbling down beside.
A dance begins with twirls and spins,
In this green theater, laughter wins.

The owls hoot in wily delight,
Their wisdom brings a hearty light.
With every rustle, secrets spill,
Nature's humor, a joyous thrill.

So gather 'round in this leafy place,
Where the sun and giggles interlace.
In every corner, laughter gleams,
A world alive with silly dreams.

Delightful Shenanigans among the Branches

Amidst the boughs where shadows play,
The critters laugh and romp all day.
A squirrel slips, a clumsy flight,
And lands with flair, what a sight!

The birds engage in playful taunts,
As wind and feathers twist and flaunt.
Branches sway with joyful glee,
A stage set for their comedy.

With every chirp, a jest unfolds,
The mischief here, a tale retold.
In leafy branches, joys collide,
With giggles echoing, far and wide.

So join the frolic, leave your gloom,
In this green realm, let laughter bloom.
Among the branches, life's a jest,
Nature's magic is truly the best.

Nature's Trickster in the Woodlands' Embrace

In the woods where the shadows prance,
A chipmunk leads the comic dance.
With little leaps and bounds so sly,
He tricks the fox, oh my, oh my!

The brook burbles with giggly glee,
As frogs ribbit in harmony.
Each splash a quip, each croak a tease,
Nature's laughter carried by the breeze.

A raccoon peeks with a cheeky grin,
As the sun dips down, the fun begins.
In this embrace of wood and leaf,
Every creature finds joy, never grief.

So wander here in whimsical cheer,
Where nature's tricks bring smiles near.
In the forest, jokes twirl like dust,
In every pixel, laughter is a must.

Blissful Shenanigans at Dawn's Door

At dawn's door, the world awakes,
With giggles shared, and silly shakes.
The sun tickles the sleepy skies,
A morning filled with playful sighs.

A deer dances, her steps quite spry,
While butterflies flit to say hi.
The flowers nod, in bright array,
As nature joins the morning play.

A jolly tune from the nest above,
A raucous chorus, the song of love.
Each note a chuckle, a wink, a grin,
In this lively show, all joy begins.

So step right in to this cheerful morn,
Where laughter weaves and joy is born.
At dawn's door, let spirits soar,
In this merry dance, forevermore.

Glorious Giggles among the Bustling Bees

In a field where the daisies sway,
A bumblebee fell on its way.
It buzzed with a comical tone,
Chasing shadows, oh so prone.

Laughter erupted from petals bright,
As ants danced in sheer delight.
The sun beamed, a chuckle in rays,
Nature's funny little plays.

A ladybug slipped on a leaf,
Her clumsy twirl brought everyone grief.
The grass whispered jokes to the breeze,
As butterflies joined in with ease.

With each giggle, the world seemed new,
A garden of laughter, fresh as dew.
In this joyful hive of delight,
The day turned silly, oh what a sight!

Silly Sighs Beneath the Canopy

Under branches that sway and creak,
The squirrels chatter, a comical sneak.
One dropped a nut, it rolled away,
And the others laughed in a playful fray.

A turtle tried to race the sun,
Its slow-motion moves were quite the fun.
While birds sang tunes, perched on high,
The whole forest chuckled, oh my, oh my!

There's a fox with a grin, prancing around,
With paws that dance, they bounce off the ground.
As shadows stretch and giggles soar,
Beneath the canopy, who could ask for more?

Silly sighs float on gentle air,
As nature joins in, a merry affair.
With laughter woven into the leaves,
The world spins on, as joy never leaves.

Carefree Echoes in the Thicket

In a thicket where laughter blooms,
Every bush hums with fun-filled tunes.
A raccoon slipped, tumbled, and spun,
As laughter erupted, oh what a run!

With echoes bouncing off the trees,
The whispers dance with the playful breeze.
A frog leaps high, misjudging its jump,
Landing in mud with a comical thump!

The flowers giggle with colors bright,
As bees waltz around, buzzing in flight.
A the wind carries tales of the day,
While critters frolic, in their own way.

In this merry glen, joy's the decree,
Nature's laughter, wild and free.
With carefree echoes in every nook,
Life's simple pleasures, all it took!

Whimsy Rides the Gentle Breeze

Whimsy rides on a feathered whim,
As clouds play tag on the sun's rim.
A kitten chased its own little tail,
While grasshoppers joined with a silly trail.

With a wink, the daisies danced in array,
Even the trees seemed to sway and play.
A bunny hopped, tripped, and fell flat,
But giggles arose, no need for a spat.

In this waved world of jolly delight,
Even shadows seem to giggle in light.
With each twist of breeze, joy takes flight,
Painting smiles through day and night.

So come join the fun, and let worries cease,
With whimsy around, there's only peace.
In laughter's embrace, we find our call,
In this merry dance, we rise and we fall!

Beneath the Open Sky

In fields of green, we trip and fall,
With laughter echoing, we lose it all.
The cows look on, in pure delight,
As we chase shadows, in morning light.

A picnic spread, but ants invade,
We put on hats with grand charades.
Silly faces, we pull them tight,
As the sun beats down, oh what a sight!

Bubbles float up, we reach too high,
One pops loudly — oh my, oh my!
A tumble here, a spill on that,
As friends all gather, each silly brat.

With hopes of fun, we dance around,
As giggles rise from the grassy ground.
Beneath the sky that's painted blue,
We find our joy in all we do.

Harmonies of Hilarity

The whip-poor-will echoes at night,
While we sing loudly, lacking all fright.
Our voices clash in a jumbled song,
Off-key and out, but it feels so wrong.

A squirrel joins in, it seems to cheer,
We nod along, our hearts full of cheer.
With each silly note, the moonlight gleams,
And laughter spills like flowing streams.

The bush shakes wildly, what could it be?
Oh look, it's just a wild bumblebee!
We dance around, dodging its flight,
Squealing with joy, in sheer delight.

With every chuckle, our spirits rise,
Under starlit skies, we don't disguise.
In the harmony of silly sounds,
We find our peace in laughter found.

Unraveled at Dawn

Morning breaks with a goofy grin,
Pajamas on, let the fun begin!
The toast burns black, smoke fills the air,
As we laugh like fools, without a care.

The cat jumps high, lands in the mug,
We erupt in giggles, cozy and snug.
Pouring tea with that clumsy flair,
We spill it, of course, but who would care?

As the sun peaks over the tree,
We bounce around, so wild and free.
Chasing our shadows in playful race,
With wobbly steps and a silly face.

Time ticks on, but we stay behind,
In tangled joy, our hearts aligned.
For in the morning's delightful mess,
We find our laughter, truly blessed.

The Unexpected Serenade

Upon a hill, we make our stand,
With pots and pans, a band so grand.
The neighbors frown, but we don't mind,
In our joyful jumbles, harmony we find.

A whistle here, and a crash right there,
A pickle jar bounces, we hardly care.
With kazoos and laughter, we make a scene,
In our silly world, we're all so keen.

The dog joins in, barking along,
With howls that prove he thinks he's strong.
With every note, the sun starts to set,
And golden rays spark joy, no regret.

As the stars peek out, we end our tune,
Beneath the glow of a pearly moon.
In unexpected moments, we find our glee,
In melodies woven, wild and free.

Splinters of Glee Among the Trees

In the forest, branches sway,
A squirrel drops a nut today.
It bounces off a log, oh dear!
We crack up, hooting with cheer.

A rabbit hops, then takes a slip,
A tumble that makes us all gip.
He shakes himself with such a glance,
We can't help but join in the dance.

The owl watches, amused, a hoot,
As friends trip over each other's foot.
Sunshine dapples on the ground,
In laughter, joy is found all around.

With each stumble, a giggle grows,
Nature's fun, as everyone knows.
In the clearing where chuckles rise,
Splinters of glee in sunny skies.

Mirth and Mayhem in the Sunlight

Underneath the golden rays,
Laughter fills the summer days.
A clumsy deer trips on a vine,
And suddenly, it's all divine.

A picnic spread, but anties swarm,
In a frenzy, they create a storm.
Fighting them off, we stifle glee,
What a comical calamity!

A bird swoops down, steals a treat,
We watch in shock, then stomp our feet.
The trees are shaking, laughter loud,
Mirth and mayhem: we're so proud!

In the sunlit woods, we play and sing,
Joy cascades through every fling.
Each moment bursts with silly delight,
In a world where all feels right.

Serenade of Smiles in the Woods

Beneath the boughs, where shadows dance,
A chipmunk pauses, taking a chance.
He fumblingly drops his berry treat,
Chasing it leaves him beat.

Nearby, a couple tries to pose,
But finds their smiles are hard to close.
With every click, a funny face,
In the serene woods, we find our place.

The rustle of leaves serves as a tune,
Creating a symphony, a playful boon.
With nature as our jolly guide,
We serenade the world wide-eyed.

Giggles bubble, frolic is near,
In the woods, we laugh without fear.
Together we roam, hearts all aglow,
Here's to the joy, let laughter flow.

Unraveled Peace in the Verge

In a patch where wildflowers bloom,
Frogs croak songs to lift the gloom.
One jumps high, then goes astray,
Landing in a puddle—what a play!

The bees zoom by in dizzy swirls,
Chasing a dream, their buzz unfurls.
A gentle breeze makes branches sway,
Sending a hat flying away!

Giggles erupt from every nook,
As kids begin to take a look.
Finding wonder in silly sights,
Unraveled peace in wild delights.

With every chuckle, tension fades,
In the verge, where joy cascades.
Nature's humor all around,
In every laugh, true bliss is found.

Elysian Echoes of Laughter

Underneath the sun so bright,
A squirrel dances in delight.
With acorns flying here and there,
Quirky moments fill the air.

A bird's song trills a funny tune,
As bees buzz round a dandelion bloom.
A rabbit trips on tangled grass,
While giggles sneakily pass.

A butterfly winks, it's quite absurd,
As if it knows the silliest word.
The trees all sway in comical sway,
Joining in this merry play.

With echoes ringing brightly through,
Nature's laughter joins the crew.
In this happy place, we roam,
Sharing smiles, we feel at home.

Melodies of the Mirthful

In the meadow where joy is found,
Laughter leaps from mound to mound.
Flowers wiggle in the breeze,
Tickled by the playful tease.

A toad croaks a silly tune,
Dancing under the watchful moon.
Crickets chirp with glee and cheer,
Mirth puts worries far from here.

Clouds play peek-a-boo with rays,
Chasing shadows in a daze.
Each moment shared brings a grin,
As joy spills out and flows within.

With every giggle, joy expands,
Nature's band joins in demands.
Harmony of heart and earth,
This merry world, a place of worth.

Whispers of Laughter in the Glade

In the glade where starlight gleams,
The trees start sharing their wild dreams.
A chipmunk jests, a playful jest,
As smiles spread through nature's nest.

Mice take turns in a little race,
Puffing cheeks, creating space.
A turtle chuckles, slow but sly,
Sinking back as time goes by.

Amidst the ferns so lush and green,
The strangest sights are often seen.
A hedgehog wears a tiny hat,
As laughter rings from here to that.

The whispers dance like leaves in flight,
In this glade, all feels just right.
With every chuckle, spirits lift,
In nature's arms, laughter is a gift.

Echoes of Joy Beneath the Canopy

Beneath the shade, the laughter rolls,
As silly antics take their tolls.
A raccoon juggles shiny stones,
With joyful shouts and playful groans.

In the canopy where shadows play,
Frogs perform in their own ballet.
Fireflies twinkle, a dazzling show,
With every flash, the smiles grow.

A wind that tickles through the trees,
Carries notes of giggles on the breeze.
Laughter ripples through the leaves,
As every critter dances, it deceives.

Echoes of happiness fill the space,
In this verdant, joy-filled place.
With every chuckle, we unite,
In this haven, everything's alright.

Fractured Silence under Open Skies

In the meadow where giggles bloom,
A cow sneezes—chaos breaks the gloom.
With butterflies caught in a jittery dance,
The sun beams down, giving laughter a chance.

A squirrel drops acorns, they roll and they crash,
Chasing each other in a frantic dash.
Laughter spills like water from a jug,
As ants march by, all snug as a bug.

A lizard laughs, tail flicking in jest,
While rabbits play hide and seek, at their best.
The wind whispers secrets, tickling the trees,
And everyone joins in, as light as the breeze.

Under the open skies, joy takes flight,
Where each little blunder seems just right.
So let's raise a cheer for this comic scene,
Nature's own circus, wild and serene.

Chuckles Among the Wildflowers

A bumblebee buzzes with a chuckling sound,
As daisies sway, they begin spinning round.
Each petal a laugh, each stem a good friend,
In this garden of giggles, the joy has no end.

The butterflies tumble, a colorful mess,
Doing the cha-cha in floral dress.
The sunbeams are dancing, a bright finale,
While daisies are planning a wildflower rally.

A rabbit hops madly, with some flair and grace,
Tripping on roots, saves face with a face!
With every small stumble, a funny new tale,
While ladybugs giggle on a snail's polished trail.

In wildflower fields, where humor does bloom,
Nature's own laughter dispels any gloom.
So join in the frolic, let go of your dread,
And smile at the wonders, where laughter is bred.

Shattered Calm in the Meadow

The calm of the meadow, shattered by quirks,
A donkey rolls over, and mischief works.
Nearby, the grass whispers jokes to the trees,
While crickets perform, swaying in the breeze.

A goat on a mission leaps high with a cheer,
As flowers erupt in giggles severe.
The clouds chuckle softly, puffing up large,
As shadows play games, becoming the charge.

A picnic gone wrong, with sandwiches tossed,
As squirrels sneak in, laughter is embossed.
An ant with a crumb—quite proud of his find,
Dances through chaos, so silly and blind.

The meadow's been laughing, under skies so bright,
With every immense blunder, delight takes flight.
Join in this frenzy, raise your voice high,
For joy freely flows beneath the wide sky.

Rays of Humor in the Clearing

In a sun-drenched clearing, laughter ignites,
Where chipmunks recite their comedic fights.
With sunflowers nodding as nature's own crowd,
Every cackle around seems pure and proud.

A hawk swoops down, makes a feathery mess,
While grasshoppers chirp, enjoying the excess.
The puddles reflect all the giggles above,
Creating ripples of joy, stories we love.

A squirrel with acorns conducts a fine show,
While clouds drift by, putting on their own glow.
In every soft rustle, the humor is there,
As each little moment invites us to share.

So gather and chuckle in this bright escape,
For each tiny mishap, a laugh to reshape.
Under the vast heavens where sunshine will beam,
Let's laugh with the world, in this shared happy dream.

Radiant Rhapsody

In a forest bright and lively,
The squirrels danced with glee,
Chasing shadows, oh so sprightly,
Their antics wild and free.

A turtle tried to join the fun,
But fell flat on his shell,
He laughed and said, 'I'm not the one!'
Then shared stories he knew well.

The rabbits hopped with flair and style,
While birds chirped songs divine,
Every creature wore a smile,
In this woodland, oh so fine.

As night fell softly, stars appeared,
They winked down at the trees,
With laughter ringing loud and weird,
Nature's band played with ease.

Frothy Laughter Among the Trees

The brook babbled jokes and puns,
   While frogs croaked out a tune,
Sunlight splashed like playful runs,
   A merry dance with noon.

The owls rolled their wise old eyes,
   As raccoons made a scene,
Sipping nectar, oh what a surprise,
   With giggles, crisp and clean.

A deer tried to perform a trick,
   But tripped over a root,
She laughed so hard, it made her sick,
   In this leafy, joyous suit.

The trees joined in, with rustling leaves,
   Like whispers of delight,
In nature's play, none grieves,
   For laughter rules the night.

Jests Beneath the Stars

Under a sky of sparkling dreams,
Fireflies lit up the scene,
With whispers, giggles, silly schemes,
Each moment felt like a screen.

A bear with a bowtie, grand and stout,
Told tales of honey and bees,
With laughter, the friends let out a shout,
Mapping secrets of the trees.

A raccoon stole a pie from the bees,
He danced away with flair,
Yet tripped and fell among the leaves,
Leaving crumbs and a squeaky air.

The night wore on with silly jokes,
While crickets played their part,
In the laughter of woodland folks,
Joy lingered, light and smart.

Brightest Shadows of Joy

Where the sunbeams play hide and seek,
And whispers tickle the ground,
The shadows giggle, never meek,
In joy they twist around.

A hedgehog donned a tiny hat,
With laughter in every spire,
He rolled and wobbled, oh how he sat,
In a game of woodland choir.

A wise old toad, with a grin so wide,
Brought stories of faraway lands,
Every creature soon complied,
Cackling, joining his hands.

With petals falling soft and light,
In mirth, they danced till dawn,
In the sweetest glow of night,
Where joy and laughter are drawn.

Humor Wrapped in Leaves

A squirrel with a hat, so dapper and spry,
Dances on branches, beneath the blue sky.
He trips on a twig, does a comical flip,
Lands in a puddle, oh what a quip!

The wind steals his hat, it's a marvelous sight,
The critters all laugh, oh what pure delight!
A bird whistles tunes, like a laugh at a joke,
As laughter erupts, the world's just bespoke.

Caterpillars giggle, hiding in green,
Watching the antics, what a hilarious scene.
With nature as jest, there's no room for frowns,
In this leafy laughter, we smother our crowns.

So let's join the jesters, in nature's grand show,
Where joy fills the air, and the humor will grow.
With leaves as our laughter, we'll sing and we'll sway,
In this whimsical grove, come dance the day away.

The Lightness of Being Under the Canopy

Under the branches, a tickle in the air,
A rabbit tells jokes, in the soft morning glare.
His punchlines bounce high, like a leaf downhill,
With giggles resounding, the world feels so shrill.

A turtle in shades, slow-moving but spry,
Makes witticisms stir, as the ants pass him by.
His shell is a stage, for the jokes he will tell,
In this lightness of being, all's jolly and well.

The branches above, in a wobbly sway,
Seem to chuckle along as the creatures all play.
With laughter as roots, we're all free to roam,
In this canopy grand, we've all found a home.

So laugh with the breeze, let your worries take flight,
In this woodland of whimsy, everything's bright.
Under the laughter, there's room for us all,
Where the lightness of being is a captivating call.

Smiles Swirling in the Soft Breeze

With every breeze that tickles the grass,
Come smiles round the bend, like a top-spinning mass.
A butterfly twirls, in a waltzy ballet,
While flowers nod along, in a jubilant sway.

The brook joins the fun, with a bubbling cheer,
Echoing laughter, as wildlife draws near.
A raccoon with a grin, steals snacks on the sly,
While the owl up above feigns a serious sigh.

Leaves rustle in chorus, a tickling sound,
Jokes whispered by breezes, all merry around.
The meadow bursts forth, with giggles and glee,
In this swirling of smiles, so wild and so free.

So dance with the shadows, let your laughter resound,
With the earth humming softly, such joy will abound.
Each moment's a treasure, so grab it and seize,
As smiles swirl together, in this soft, playful breeze.

Witty Whispers in the Woodland

In a glade full of whispers, the trees spill their jokes,
While critters convene, sharing laughs with the folks.
A plucky old fox, with a grin oh so wide,
Winks at the crowd, as the laughter won't hide.

Every twig holds a story, a quip in the leaves,
While beetles debate, beneath shadows of eves.
A raccoon's sly glance, it's a riddle he spins,
As the chuckles erupt, like the breeze in the bins.

Moss cushions the ground, where smiles come to play,
In the heart of the woods, there's a light-filled ballet.
Where laughter is currency, barter with ease,
Each chortle a gift, in this woodland of tease.

So gather your friends, let the echoes convene,
In this witty haven, where the sun's ever keen.
With whispers of folly, let the merriment start,
In the laughter-filled woodland, we hold with our heart.